SPACE DISCOVERY GUIDES

ASTRONAUTS

A SPACE DISCOVERY GUIDE

Margaret J. Goldstein

Lerner Publications ◆ Minneapolis

Lerner Publications Company
A division of Lerner Publishing Group, Inc.
241 First Avenue North
Minneapolis, MN 55401 USA

For reading levels and more information, look up this title
at www.lernerbooks.com.

Main body text set in Avenir LT Std 65 Medium 11.5/17.5.
Typeface provided by Adobe Systems.

Library of Congress Cataloging-in-Publication Data

Names: Goldstein, Margaret J.
Title: Astronauts : a space discovery guide / Margaret J.
    Goldstein.
Description: Minneapolis : Lerner Publications, [2017] |
    Series: Space discovery guides | Audience: Age 9–12.
    | Audience: Grade 4 to 6. | Includes bibliographical
    references and index.
Identifiers: LCCN 2016016351 (print) | LCCN 2016016669
    (ebook) | ISBN 9781512425888 (lb : alk. paper) |
    ISBN 9781512427936 (eb pdf)
Subjects: LCSH: Astronauts—Juvenile literature. | Manned
    space flight—History—Juvenile literature. | Space
    flight—Juvenile literature.
Classification: LCC TL855 .G65 2017 (print) | LCC TL855
    (ebook) | DDC 629.45009—dc23

LC record available at https://lccn.loc.gov/2016016351

Manufactured in the United States of America
1-41356-23300-6/24/2016

TABLE OF CONTENTS

INTRODUCTION

HIGH FLIERS

Space shuttle *Atlantis* takes off from the Kennedy Space Center in Florida.

When you hear the word *astronaut*, you might think of rumbling rockets blasting skyward, lifting humans into space. You might think of men and women floating in space in bulky space suits. Or perhaps you envision people walking on the moon. You probably don't think about vegetable gardens when you hear the word *astronaut*—but you should. That's because high overhead, about 248 miles (399 kilometers) above Earth, on a spacecraft called the International Space Station (ISS), astronauts are growing lettuce and other vegetables under indoor lights. In August 2015, US astronauts ate space-grown food for the first time.

This lettuce was grown in space.

Why grow gardens in space? Everyone needs fresh vegetables to stay healthy, and astronauts are no different. Unpiloted cargo vehicles often deliver supplies to the ISS. The deliveries include fresh fruits and vegetables. But the ISS has no refrigerators for food, so astronauts eat the fresh foods right away. Then astronauts return to a diet of freeze-dried, packaged foods—plus some veggies grown on board.

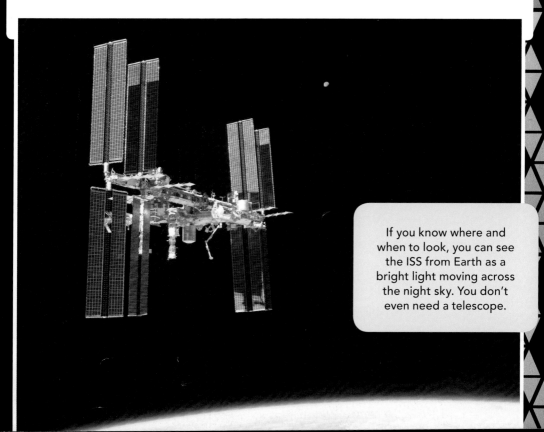

If you know where and when to look, you can see the ISS from Earth as a bright light moving across the night sky. You don't even need a telescope.

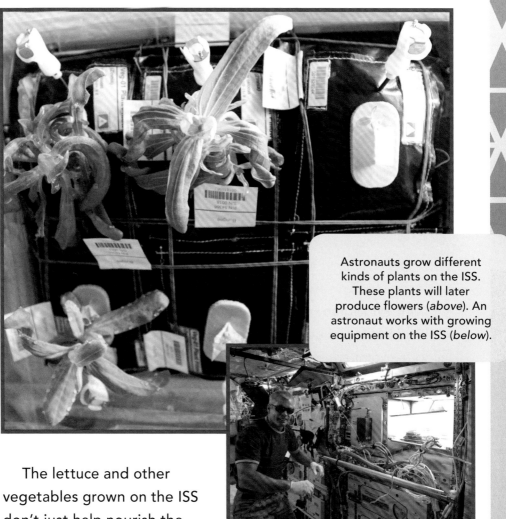

Astronauts grow different kinds of plants on the ISS. These plants will later produce flowers (*above*). An astronaut works with growing equipment on the ISS (*below*).

The lettuce and other vegetables grown on the ISS don't just help nourish the astronauts. The ISS vegetable gardens are part of an experiment. Scientists want to find the best ways to grow foods in space because the United States hopes to send astronauts on a three-year, round-trip journey to Mars. A spaceship on its way to Mars—a journey of millions of miles—couldn't be resupplied by cargo ships. Instead, astronauts would have to rely on stored, packaged foods and vegetables grown on board.

▶ OUT OF THIS WORLD

Astronauts in space face a dangerous journey. Powerful rockets blast capsules holding astronauts into orbit. Even a small mechanical failure or human miscalculation can cause an explosion during launch. The ISS and other spacecraft are safe havens for astronauts—with supplies of food and oxygen—but only if all systems are working properly. One mishap—anything from an oxygen leak to a collision with space debris—can spell doom for an astronaut crew. And the trip back home is a bumpy, fiery journey through Earth's atmosphere, requiring split-second decision making for a safe landing. More than twenty astronauts have been killed in accidents before or during space travel.

Italian astronaut Samantha Cristoforetti smiles for the camera aboard the ISS (*left*). The station is packed full of complex systems that astronauts must maintain to stay safe and complete their missions (*above*).

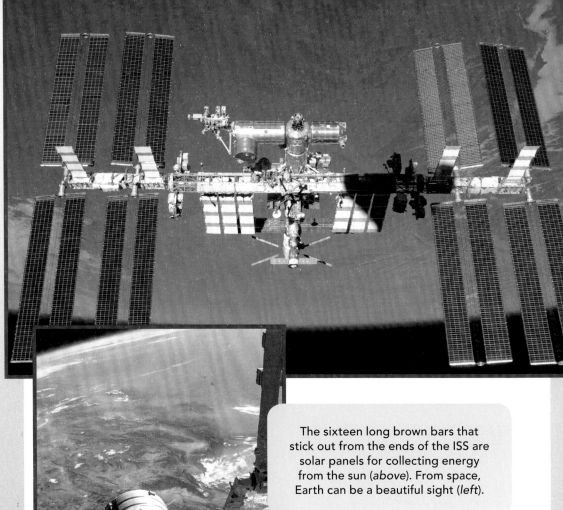

The sixteen long brown bars that stick out from the ends of the ISS are solar panels for collecting energy from the sun (*above*). From space, Earth can be a beautiful sight (*left*).

Most astronauts say that the joys of space travel make all the risks worthwhile. From space, astronauts have a breathtaking view of Earth. They can see swirling clouds, vast expanses of blue oceans, sprawling cities, and varied land formations. And astronauts in space become familiar with something that few humans ever experience: weightlessness, or zero gravity. In space, astronauts do not feel the pull of Earth's gravity. In space there is no up or down.

This astronaut is having fun with some fruit in space.

Objects that would be impossible for a person to lift on Earth weigh nothing in space. Canadian astronaut Chris Hadfield, who has made several visits to the ISS, describes the magical experience: "You can move huge objects with the flick of a wrist, hang upside down from the ceiling like a bat, tumble through the air like an Olympic gymnast. You can *fly*."

CHAPTER 1
UP, UP, AND AWAY

Yuri Gagarin

Since 1961 about 550 people have traveled into space. The first was Yuri Gagarin of the former Soviet Union (a nation, based in modern-day Russia, that existed from 1922 to 1991). In 1961 this cosmonaut (the Russian name for astronaut) orbited Earth in a capsule called *Vostok 1*. Less than a year after Gagarin's trip, the United States sent astronaut John Glenn into orbit. The first person to move around outside of a ship in space, called spacewalking, was cosmonaut Alexei Leonov, in 1965.

John Glenn smiles during training for his first spaceflight.

Space exploration reached a thrilling milestone on July 20, 1969, when US astronauts Neil Armstrong and then Buzz Aldrin became the first humans to walk on the moon. The United States sent astronauts to the moon five more times between 1969 and 1972.

In the late twentieth century, the United States built a fleet of space shuttles. These craft, which operated from 1981 to 2011, were launched into space by rockets and landed like airplanes. The shuttles carried astronauts into space to repair satellites, conduct experiments, and make observations of Earth and the solar system.

Buzz Aldrin walks on the moon in 1969 with the US flag visible in the distance. The flag is still on the surface of the moon.

Shuttles also carried astronauts to Mir, a Soviet space station that operated from 1986 to 2001. The space shuttle era was marked by two tragedies. The shuttle *Challenger* exploded on takeoff in 1986. Its seven crew members were killed. The shuttle *Columbia* broke apart on reentry in 2003. That accident also killed all seven crew members.

In the late 1990s, the United States and fourteen other nations began to build the International Space Station. Space agencies hired aerospace

Workers built the ISS's parts and modules on Earth (*above*). In space, astronauts assembled the pieces to create the space station (*below*).

companies to construct the station's parts and machinery on Earth. Shuttles carried the materials into space, where teams of astronauts assembled them. This work involved a lot of spacewalking. The station was ready in November 2000. Astronauts from different nations have occupied it ever since.

▶ THE RIGHT STUFF

In the United States, the National Aeronautics and Space Administration (NASA) is in charge of astronauts and their missions. Many people want to become astronauts. When NASA advertised for new astronauts in late 2015 and early 2016, more than eighteen thousand Americans applied for the job.

NASA sets high standards for astronauts. To even be considered, an applicant must have a college degree in engineering, biological science, physical science, or mathematics.

NASA accepts only highly skilled professionals to train for a trip to space.

In addition, a candidate must have at least three years of job experience related to his or her college degree or must have logged at least one thousand hours piloting a jet aircraft. Candidates must also be physically fit, with normal blood pressure and good eyesight (although eyeglasses or surgery to correct common vision problems are allowed). To make sure that astronauts fit into space vehicles and space suits, NASA even puts limits on the size of astronauts. No one taller than 6 foot 3 (1.9 meters) can travel into space.

From the eighteen thousand–plus applications NASA received in 2015 and 2016, the agency will choose only eight to fourteen people to join its astronaut ranks. They will enter an elite club. In 2015 NASA employed only forty-seven active astronauts.

► LEARNING CURVES

Astronauts must learn to pilot a space capsule, repair machinery on spacecraft, operate robotic equipment, and conduct scientific experiments. Some astronauts never leave Earth. Their work

An astronaut training for a trip to the ISS

Astronauts sit at the controls of a simulator. Modern technology has made simulators more realistic and useful than ever.

US astronaut Scott Kelly trained for years for his space missions.

involves planning, assisting, and evaluating space missions from the ground. Other astronauts visit space only once in a career, while others make repeated trips into space.

Training for a space voyage can take between two and four years. During this time, astronauts practice over and over again the tasks they will perform in space. They work inside simulators, which are full-scale mock-ups of the spacecraft they'll use on a mission. The simulators include all the controls and data monitors that an astronaut will encounter inside a real spacecraft. Simulators also offer computer-generated views similar to what astronauts will see through spacecraft windows.

Astronauts in space suits train underwater.

Inside simulators, astronauts practice taking off from the launchpad, orbiting Earth, docking with the ISS, and returning to Earth. They also prepare for mishaps that might occur along the way.

Astronauts practice spacewalks by donning full space suits (including oxygen tanks) and spending hours in a giant swimming pool near the Johnson Space Center in Houston, Texas. The pool gives astronauts a sensation that's similar to weightlessness. Underwater, the

The training pool is 40 feet (12 m) deep and holds 6.2 million gallons (23 million liters) of water.

fully suited astronauts practice the precise movements they will use to install equipment, make repairs, and perform other tasks on a spacewalk.

Astronauts preparing for a mission spend a lot of time in the classroom. They study astronomy, meteorology, robotics, and orbital mechanics—the science of how rockets and other objects in space move under the influence of gravity. They need to know how to survive in a crash on land or water. So they attend wilderness survival training.

▶ BLAST OFF!

Before a space mission, astronauts travel to their launch sites. There, doctors give astronauts thorough medical exams. NASA doesn't want to send sick astronauts to the ISS, where they could easily infect the rest of the crew.

After passing their medical tests, astronauts go into quarantine, or isolation, for about two weeks. Quarantine shields astronauts from germs that might get them sick. They stay inside ultraclean buildings. Family members who come to say good-bye talk to them through glass, with no physical contact

Astronauts wave good-bye from their launch site.

allowed. These rules prevent outsiders from passing on sickness to astronauts.

On launch day, astronauts don helmeted space suits to protect them in an emergency. The suits are flame resistant and able to float. They can provide astronauts with emergency supplies of oxygen. Space capsules and other space vehicles are pressurized— the air inside them presses on astronauts' bodies with the same force that air presses on people on the ground. Without the correct amount of pressure, people in space can get sick or even die. Space suits are pressurized too. If a space capsule accidentally loses air pressure, pressurized space suits can save the astronauts.

Until 2011 US astronauts traveled in space shuttles, which usually carried five to seven crew members. After the shuttle fleet was retired, NASA arranged to fly its astronauts to the ISS in Russian Soyuz space capsules. These vehicles are much smaller than space shuttles, with room

Astronaut Tim Peake of the European Space Agency wears a space suit during training for a mission.

for only three people. Astronauts climb stairs and then take an elevator to reach the Soyuz capsule, which sits on top of a bundle of rockets.

Before takeoff in a space capsule, astronauts lie on their backs in a compartment called the descent module. Technicians strap them tightly into their seats. The astronauts and mission controllers on the ground run through a long checklist, making sure that all equipment and systems are operating correctly. Finally, mission controllers fire the rocket engines and the capsule powers skyward.

Space missions require the efforts of many people, including these mission managers.

A Soyuz capsule in space

New Rides

Since the space shuttles retired in 2011, NASA has sent astronauts to the ISS in Russian spacecraft, launched from the Republic of Kazakhstan, formerly part of the Soviet Union. But the United States wants its own space vehicles once again. So in 2014, NASA hired two US aerospace companies—Boeing and SpaceX—to build new spacecraft. The vehicles, Boeing's *CST-100* and SpaceX's *Crew Dragon*, will be ready to fly in 2017 or 2018. They'll launch from the United States.

In the past, NASA owned and controlled all its own space vehicles. But in the deal with Boeing and SpaceX, the private companies will own the craft. NASA will pay the companies to carry astronauts and cargo to the ISS on the new vehicles. Boeing and SpaceX might also use the vehicles for space tourism and other space projects.

NASA is also building its own new spacecraft called *Orion*. The craft is designed for long space journeys, such as a trip to Mars. NASA hopes to have *Orion* ready for launch in the early 2020s. A rocket called the Space Launch System will carry *Orion* into space.

This illustration shows how the *Orion* spacecraft may look.

Rockets launch a Soyuz capsule into space.

As the craft climbs higher, the rockets separate from the crew compartments at set intervals and fall back to Earth. As the vehicle speeds up, astronauts feel about three times the normal force of gravity pushing down on their bodies. About nine minutes into the flight, the craft reaches Earth's orbit. Space crews usually bring a small toy or doll into the descent module. When the object begins to drift upward, astronauts know they have obtained weightlessness.

CHAPTER 2
HOME IN SPACE

Soyuz capsules are designed to dock with the ISS.

With their capsule in orbit, astronauts head toward their destination in space. During the space shuttle era, astronauts carried out various missions, such as repairing satellites and the Hubble Space Telescope. During the Soyuz era, astronauts head only to the International Space Station. In space, the Soyuz capsule is solar powered, with energy provided by the sun. The trip to the ISS can take as little as three hours, but most craft orbit for a day or two before docking. During this time, astronauts adjust to weightlessness and make preparations for docking.

During orbit, astronauts move from the Soyuz launch and descent module into a van-sized compartment called the orbital module. There they can stretch their legs and sleep. The inner ear, the organ in the human body that controls balance, gets confused by the new sensation of weightlessness. Many astronauts become nauseated and vomit when they go into orbit.

Automated systems guide the capsule to its dock on the ISS. After docking, astronauts travel through a hatch into their new home in space. The structure is made of many modules connected by passageways. Altogether, the station is as large as a football field, including both end zones. The interior offers more space than a five-bedroom home. But it doesn't look much like a home. The modules are crammed full of scientific equipment, computers, electrical wires, and machines.

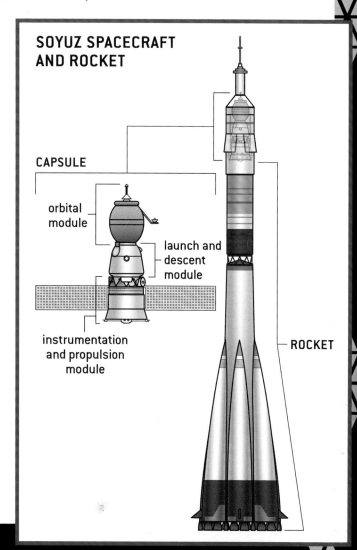

SOYUZ SPACECRAFT AND ROCKET

CAPSULE

orbital module

launch and descent module

instrumentation and propulsion module

ROCKET

Many walls are lined with strips of Velcro. Astronauts fasten tools and other supplies to the Velcro to keep them from floating around in zero gravity.

ESSENTIALS

Imagine trying to cook dinner and having all the ingredients, bowls, knives, and other utensils drift off the counter and float around this way and that. That's what would happen if you tried to cook on the ISS. So astronauts in space eat foods that don't require much preparation. Some of this food is dehydrated, or dried. Astronauts add a bit of water to restore it to its normal texture. Whenever astronauts on the ISS open food packages, they make sure that the contents don't escape and drift around the kitchen. They use straws to drink liquid out of sealed pouches. Astronauts don't eat ordinary bread,

With no gravity, everyday tasks such as eating meals can be challenging.

since the crumbs would float around and perhaps muck up station equipment. Instead, astronauts eat a lot of tortillas, which don't make a mess in zero gravity. Astronauts on the ISS also eat lots of sticky foods such as cheese spreads, peanut butter, applesauce, and pudding. These moist foods stick to tortillas, spoons, and serving containers. Although NASA menu planners try to send a variety of healthful foods to the ISS, astronauts report that many foods taste bland in space. With no gravity to pull body fluids toward their feet, astronauts usually have stuffy noses. This congestion interferes with the sense of taste.

Astronauts use straws and enclosed containers for drinking to prevent liquid from floating around the capsule.

Astronauts have water on the ISS, but it doesn't flow from faucets. It is stored in big containers, and astronauts are very careful to keep it contained to prevent water from drifting around their modules. Instead of taking showers, astronauts clean themselves with wet, soapy cloths. Water is heavy, and transporting it from Earth to the ISS is expensive. So astronauts recycle all the water used on the station, even water from their own breath, sweat, and urine. They run the dirty water through machines that clean it.

Toilets on the ISS are equipped with handholds and footholds. These keep astronauts from floating off the toilet seat. Astronauts urinate into a tube that sucks up the liquid and sends it on to the station's water recycling equipment. They defecate into a toilet that flushes with air instead of water.

At bedtime, astronauts retire inside small sleep pods. Each pod contains a sleeping bag, which is tied to the wall at one end. Astronauts don't lie on mattresses or rest their heads on pillows. They simply climb inside their sleeping bags and float.

BODY AND SOUL

The human body wasn't designed for weightlessness. In space, with no pull of gravity, astronauts' muscles weaken, hearts shrink, and bones get less dense. To counteract some of these

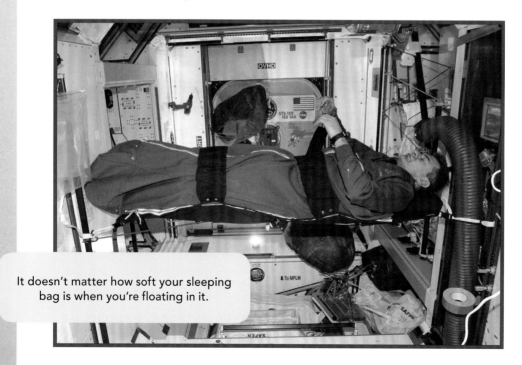

It doesn't matter how soft your sleeping bag is when you're floating in it.

effects, astronauts on the ISS exercise for at least two hours a day, six days a week. They work out on stationary bikes, treadmills, and weight-lifting machines. The equipment has straps and harnesses to hold the astronauts in place in zero gravity. Harnesses, backpacks, and bungee cords also create resistance—the sensation that astronauts are actually carrying, pulling, and pushing heavy loads.

The ISS is divided into a Russian section and a US section. Astronauts from Canada, Japan, and European nations sometimes work on the US side. Usually about six astronauts live on the ISS at once. They share meals and keep one another company. Astronauts also communicate with mission controllers and with family at home via phone, video feeds, e-mail, and radio. Astronauts use

Exercise is important for everyone, but it's especially important for astronauts to work out in space to prevent health problems (top). Astronauts from five countries pose for a photo on the ISS (bottom).

This astronaut is eyeing the chessboard from every angle.

Astronauts kick back to watch a movie on the ISS.

digital tablets and laptop computers for both work and pleasure. They relax with music on CDs, movies on DVDs, books, and musical instruments.

From the ISS, astronauts can see stars, the moon, planets, and earthly wonders such as the northern lights. Astronauts say that the views of Earth and space from the ISS are breathtaking. The station travels around 17,100 miles (27,520 km) per hour. At this speed,

The northern lights (*above*) and a sunrise (*below*) as seen from the ISS

it orbits Earth once every ninety minutes. It passes from darkness into sunshine and back into darkness sixteen times a day. So astronauts on the ISS see sixteen sunrises and sixteen sunsets every day. This phenomenon has its drawbacks, however. The changing light disrupts the body's natural sleep rhythms, making it difficult for astronauts to get a good night's sleep. NASA engineers are working on lighting technology to help solve this problem.

Scott Kelly performs an experiment aboard the ISS.

The ISS is a working research laboratory. Astronauts on the station conduct experiments, collect data, and send the data back to scientists on Earth for analysis. For example, astronauts on the ISS in 2015 and 2016 tested the use of inflatable space habitats (living quarters), analyzed how microscopic organisms behave in space, and studied how protein crystals respond to zero gravity.

Some experiments on the ISS involve the astronauts themselves. Scientists want a better understanding of how

Astronauts study the way their bodies react to weightlessness with a series of tests.

spaceflight changes the human body, so they study astronauts in space. In 2013 astronauts measured one another's eye pressure and ran ultrasound scans on one another's hands, spines, and hearts. Medical experts on the ground guided the astronauts through the procedures. The astronauts also collected and ran tests on their own urine and blood samples and sent the data to scientists on Earth.

Samantha Cristoforetti working with complex medical equipment in space. Notice that she has her feet hooked under a bar to keep from floating away.

One Twin in Space, One on Earth

On March 28, 2015, Scott Kelly blasted off in a Russian space capsule, along with cosmonaut Mikhail Kornienko. They returned to Earth on March 1, 2016. Kelly's 340-day stay in space is the longest for any US astronaut.

During Kelly's time on the ISS, scientists studied his health, including his sleep patterns, vision, blood, and immune system. The scientists wanted a better understanding of how long-term spaceflight affects astronauts' bodies. This research will be especially important in preparing for a three-year round-trip mission to Mars.

Scott Kelly has an identical twin brother, Mark Kelly. He is also an astronaut. During Scott Kelly's time on the ISS, Mark Kelly remained on Earth. There he underwent the same medical studies being done on his brother. Because they are twins, they have very similar bodies. Comparing the brothers' test results shows scientists very precisely how a body changes when it goes into space.

Identical twins don't just look the same. They also have identical deoxyribonucleic acid (DNA). DNA is found in the cells of all living things. It contains instructions for how living things grow, function, and reproduce. Scientists know that environmental factors can trigger changes in DNA. They are comparing the DNA of the Kelly twins to determine whether spending nearly a year in space changed Scott's DNA.

FIX-IT

The ISS contains 8 miles (13 km) of electrical wire. The US side holds forty-four computers running 1.5 million lines of software code. A 1-acre (0.4-hectare) solar panel array powers the station lights and equipment, including machines that make oxygen for the crew. With guidance from engineers on the ground, astronauts must keep all this equipment running properly and repair it when necessary. In 2014 astronauts set up a 3-D printer on the ISS. With this device, astronauts can create new metal and plastic parts for broken equipment.

A 55-foot (17 m) robotic arm does much of the exterior work on the ISS.

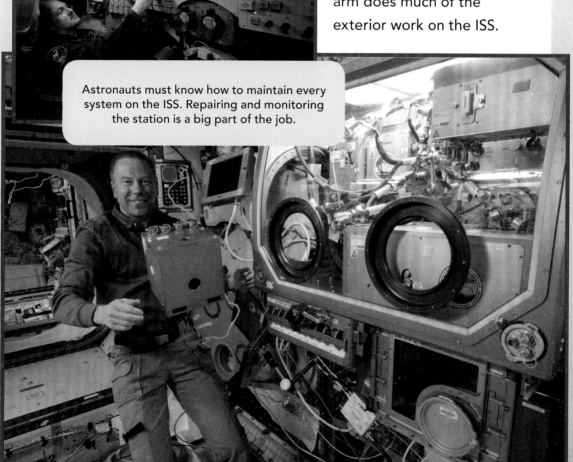

Astronauts must know how to maintain every system on the ISS. Repairing and monitoring the station is a big part of the job.

The ISS's robotic arm latches onto a cargo vehicle to pull it to the station.

It can catch and move cargo vehicles and space capsules, make repairs, and attach modules to one another. But the robot doesn't have a mind of its own. Astronauts inside the ISS control its movements, and all astronauts must know how to use it.

The robotic arm can make some fixes to the space station exterior. But some problems are trickier. They need up-close human attention. When a precision repair is needed, an astronaut must don a space suit for extravehicular activity (EVA), better known as spacewalking.

A spacewalking suit is much bulkier and more complex than the suits worn in space capsules. The spacewalking suit covers every inch of an astronaut's body. The fourteen-layer suit is pressurized and temperature controlled. It is tough enough to protect the astronaut from orbiting space debris (fragments from old satellites and other spacecraft), deadly radiation from the sun, and the sun's fierce heat. It holds an oxygen tank, a radio, and safety tethers that connect the astronaut to the spacecraft. The suit also has a backpack with small jet thrusters and a joystick. If an astronaut were to accidentally become untethered during a spacewalk, he or she could use the joystick to control the thrusters and fly back to the craft.

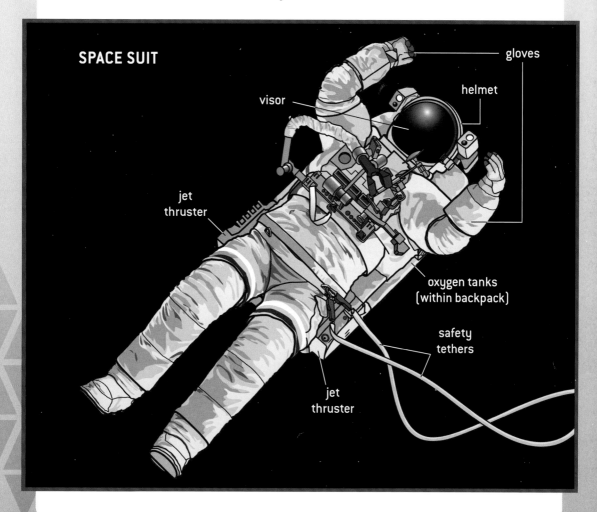

SPACE SUIT

gloves

helmet

visor

jet thruster

oxygen tanks (within backpack)

safety tethers

jet thruster

To exit the ISS for an EVA, astronauts enter an air lock. This chamber has two airtight doors. Astronauts pass through the first door and lock it behind them. Then they open the second door and leave the spacecraft. This system keeps air from escaping the ISS.

Once an astronaut is out in space, working inside the bulky space suit is extremely awkward. Astronaut Chris Hadfield says, "Just turning a wrench to loosen a bolt can be like trying to change a tire while wearing ice skates and goalie mitts." Via radio, mission controllers on Earth and astronauts inside the ISS carefully guide spacewalkers as they perform needed tasks. Spacewalks can last for hours. Once the job is done, spacewalkers reenter the ISS through the station's air lock.

Spacewalking is one of the most dangerous parts of a mission to the ISS. Threats include space junk, radiation, and mechanical failure.

COMING AND GOING

Astronauts come and go from the ISS. Groups of astronauts stay for weeks or months depending on their missions. At any given

This Soyuz capsule is docked at the ISS.

Astronauts greet each other on the ISS. Everything feels different without gravity, including hugs.

time, as few as three and as many as thirteen astronauts might be at the station. The typical number is six.

At least one Soyuz capsule is always docked at the ISS. This craft can serve as a lifeboat in an emergency. For instance, if a large piece of space debris were headed toward the ISS and the station could not get out of its way, the crew could scramble into a Soyuz and escape back to Earth. Other Soyuz capsules bring new astronauts for their missions and take home those who have finished their stays.

CHAPTER 4
DOWN TO EARTH

A Soyuz capsule floats to Earth, its mission complete.

For the trip home, astronauts put on the light space suits they wore during the trip up. They strap themselves into the descent module of a Soyuz capsule docked at the ISS. Springs on the station push the capsule into space. Then the pilot fires the capsule's engines and steers it into orbit around Earth.

More than two hours later, the astronauts fire the engines again and put the Soyuz into descent, headed toward a landing field in Kazakhstan. The craft rubs against gases in Earth's upper atmosphere, and this rubbing slows it. The rubbing also makes the Soyuz grow extremely hot. About twenty-eight minutes into the descent, the orbital module and a third section of the Soyuz, the instrumentation and propulsion module, break off from the descent module. Those sections grow fiery hot and burn up as they fall through the atmosphere.

The descent module is covered with a fireproof shield that keeps it from burning up. Inside the module, the astronauts experience a hot and rocky ride. Astronaut Scott Kelly compares it to "going over Niagara Falls in a barrel—while you're on fire." Parachutes and rockets slow the craft as it falls, but it still makes a hard landing on the plains of Kazakhstan.

REST AND RECOVERY

Astronauts usually emerge from the Soyuz dazed and dizzy. They must readjust to Earth's gravity, and the switch can disrupt balance and coordination. Many astronauts experience fatigue, body aches, and other ailments when they return to Earth. Recovery can take about one day for each day an astronaut has spent in space. One interesting side effect of weightlessness is that astronauts return to Earth several inches taller than before leaving. Without gravity, cartilage between a person's vertebrae (bones of the spine) expands. For instance, when Scott Kelly came home after nearly a year on the ISS in March

Workers prepare to pull astronauts from a Soyuz capsule after its landing in Kazakhstan.

Astronauts and their families gather after a successful Soyuz landing. Depending on the mission, they may have been apart for months.

2016, he stood about 2 inches (5 centimeters) taller than before he left. In a few days, his height returned to normal.

After a mission, NASA doctors put astronauts through extensive medical tests to evaluate the lasting effects of weightlessness on their bodies. Astronauts also spend many hours on mission debriefing. During these sessions, astronauts and NASA administrators review all the aspects of the completed mission and consider ways to improve future spaceflights.

After recovering their health, astronauts return to their Earth-based duties with NASA. They help train other astronauts, work as mission controllers, collaborate with space agencies from other nations, and handle other tasks. Some astronauts will return to space in the future. Others will spend the rest of their careers on the ground. But astronauts will always remember the thrill of living in space. US astronaut Mike Fincke recalls that thrill. He says, "A little push with your big toe will take you halfway across the station. It's like being Superman."

WHAT'S NEXT?

The last piloted moon mission took place in 1972. Since then, NASA and other space agencies have sent unpiloted space probes great distances. NASA has sent several remote-controlled rovers to explore the surface of Mars. Spacecraft have also flown past Venus, Jupiter, Uranus, Neptune, and Pluto (making observations and gathering data on the way) and continued outside the solar system. But since 1972, no astronauts have flown farther than the Hubble Space Telescope, which orbits about 380 miles (612 km) above Earth.

NASA plans to change that with future piloted missions beyond Earth's orbit. One NASA project planned for the 2020s is called the Asteroid Redirect Mission.

This photo of Nepture was taken by a *Voyager* spacecraft (*left*). The rover *Curiosity* took this selfie on Mars (*below*).

Space vehicles of the future may include the *Orion* spacecraft (*above*) and Virgin Galactic's *Unity* (*left*).

It will send a robotic vehicle to collect part of an asteroid (a rocky or metallic object orbiting the sun) and put it into orbit around the moon. After that, astronauts traveling on NASA's new *Orion* spacecraft will visit the asteroid, cut samples from it, and return them to Earth for study. By examining the asteroid up close, scientists hope to learn more about the solar system. The boldest plans for *Orion* involve a piloted mission to Mars. NASA hopes to make that trip a reality by the 2030s.

NASA isn't the only group planning to send humans into space. A company called Virgin Galactic plans to take tourists on a thrilling ride above the atmosphere. On a two-and-a-half-hour flight, passengers will experience weightlessness and get awe-inspiring views of Earth and space. About seven hundred people have already made reservations for a flight on Virgin's VSS *Unity* spacecraft. The cost for a ticket is $250,000. Other companies are planning to take tourists on similar trips. Some people even envision human colonies on the moon and Mars someday. If and when these projects ever get off the ground, one thing is certain: astronauts will lead the way.

NASA astronaut Michael L. Gernhardt during a spacewalk

Source Notes

9   Chris Hadfield, *An Astronaut's Guide to Life on Earth* (New York: Little, Brown, 2013), 200.

36   Ibid. 32.

39   Jeffrey Kluger, "A Commute Home—from Space," *Time*, March 12, 2015, http://time.com/3742272/soyuz-landing-nasa-esa.

40   Charles Fishman, "5,200 Days in Space," *Atlantic*, January/February 2015, http://www.theatlantic.com/magazine/archive/2015/01/5200-days-in -space/383510.

Glossary

aerospace: a branch of science dealing with Earth's atmosphere and the space beyond

asteroid: a rocky or metallic object orbiting the sun

astronaut: a person who pilots a spacecraft or works in space

astronomy: the study of the space and objects outside of Earth's atmosphere

atmosphere: a layer of gases surrounding a planet or another body in space

cosmonaut: an astronaut working for the former Soviet Union or for modern-day Russia

gravity: a naturally occurring force that pulls objects in space toward one another. Gravity pulls objects near Earth toward the planet. In space, astronauts do not feel the pull of Earth's gravity.

orbit: to travel around another object. For instance, the International Space Station orbits Earth. The path an object takes during this trip is also called its orbit.

pressurize: to cause the air pressure inside something, such as a space vehicle or space suit, to match the pressure of air on Earth's surface. When air pressure does not match levels found on Earth, humans can get sick and have difficulty breathing.

robotics: the design, construction, and operation of robots (mechanical devices that carry out tasks automatically)

satellite: a natural or human-made object that orbits another object in space. Human-made satellites do jobs such as studying weather, relaying communications signals, and photographing Earth from space.

simulator: a model of a vehicle, outfitted with the same controls and systems one would find in the real vehicle, used for training. Simulators of space vehicles on Earth allow astronauts to practice tasks they will perform in space.

solar power: energy derived from the sun's rays. The International Space Station is fueled by solar power.

space debris: any human-made object traveling through space that is not controlled by people on Earth. Space debris includes disabled satellites and pieces of metal, glass, and plastic that have broken off spacecraft.

Selected Bibliography

Associated Press. "Orion Launch Date Pushed Back Two Years to 2023." *Denver Post*, September 16, 2015. http://www.denverpost.com/business /ci_28823971/orion-launch-date-pushed-back-two-years-2023.

Hadfield, Chris. *An Astronaut's Guide to Life on Earth*. New York: Little, Brown, 2013.

Rincon, Paul. "Tim Peake: UK Astronaut Heads for Space Station." *BBC News*, December 15, 2015. http://www.bbc.com/news/science-environment -34991335.

"Timeline: 50 Years of Spaceflight." *Space.com*, September 28, 2012. http:// www.space.com/4422-timeline-50-years-spaceflight.html.

Further Reading and Websites

ESA Kids—Life in Space
https://www.esa.int/esaKIDSen/Livinginspace.html

Jones, Tom. *Ask the Astronaut: A Galaxy of Astonishing Answers to Your Questions on Spaceflight*. Washington, DC: Smithsonian Books, 2016.

NASA—Spot the Station
http://spotthestation.nasa.gov

NASA—Ten Things to Know about Scott Kelly's Year in Space https://www .nasa.gov/mission_pages/station/research/news/top_ten_1YM

Waxman, Laura Hamilton. *Exploring Space Travel*. Minneapolis: Lerner Publications, 2012.

———. *Exploring the International Space Station*. Minneapolis: Lerner Publications, 2012.

Index

Photo Acknowledgments

The images in this book are used with the permission of: NASA, pp. 2, 5 (all), 6 (all), 7 (right), 8 (all), 11 (all), 12 (all), 13 (all), 16 (bottom), 19 (bottom), 20, 22, 24 (all), 25, 26, 27 (all), 28 (all), 29 (bottom), 30, 31 (all), 33 (bottom), 34, 40, 41 (all), 42 (top), 43; NASA/Bill Ingalls, pp. 4, 14, 15 (bottom), 17, 19 (top), 21; ESA/ NASA, pp. 7 (left), 9, 29 (top); © Everet Collection Historical/Alamy, pp. 10; NASA/David C. Bowman, p. 15 (top); NASA/Bill Stafford, p. 16 (top); NASA/ Victor Zelentsov, p. 18; © Laura Westlund/Independent Picture Service, pp. 23, 35; AP Photo/Pat Sullivan, p. 32; ESA-S.CORVAJA, p. 33 (top); AP Photo/Krill Kudryastev, pp. 38, 39; © Ricky Carioti/The Washington Post/Getty Images, p. 42 (bottom); NASA, p. 43.

Front cover: NASA.